Virtual Reality

BEGINNER'S GUIDE

Frederic Lardinois
& Patrick Buckley

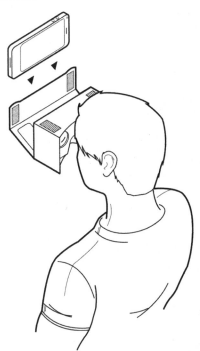

Regan Arts.

Welcome to the Virtual Reality Revolution!

What if we could escape our ordinary, sometimes boring lives and be transported into a computer-simulated, immersive, and interactive "virtual reality"? It's long been the stuff of dime-store science fiction novels, an idea that for decades has both obsessed and vexed scientists and computer programmers. But the virtual reality revolution is finally upon us. And thanks to Google's Cardboard project, it requires nothing more than a piece of cardboard, two plastic lenses, and your smartphone.

Before we step through the looking glass, perhaps we should answer the most obvious question: What exactly *is* virtual reality (VR)?

The clever folks at NASA define virtual reality as the "use of computer technology to create the effect of an interactive three-dimensional world in which the objects have a sense of spatial presence." In other words, VR is an environment generated by a computer, with depth and perspective that change as you explore and interact with it. Ideally, when using a virtual reality viewer, you should feel like you are a part of the virtual world, not just looking at it. But it's hard to trick our brains into believing that what we're seeing through a viewer is real.

The key attribute that makes VR so exciting to experience is its *immersive presence*—which convinces you that you are genuinely inhabiting a virtual space. For instance, if you're standing on a virtual cliff, it will be really, really hard for you to leap off of it—even though you know you're actually standing in your kitchen, holding your cardboard viewer to your eyes.

Google's Cardboard project and a growing number of VR apps generate immersive presence by making use of the very sophisticated sensors our smartphones now contain. The same gyroscopes and accelerometers that allow racing games to use your phone as a steering wheel also track your head's movements while you're using the cardboard viewer.

Say you are using your viewer and you tilt your head to the left. The phone's gyroscope and accelerometer register that movement, passing it on to the software and the graphics chip to calculate the image you see. The software then creates two different images—one for your left eye and one for your right eye—to provide the 3D effect. That's a pretty complicated process, and it takes even the fast graphics processors found in modern smartphones a few milliseconds per eye.

But the image still has to get to the screen. While it may seem as if images appear on the screen instantaneously, the screen actually takes a few milliseconds to change color, adding a small delay. To make you feel really immersed in a virtual world, this has to happen approximately 60 times per second for each eye. And if the latency between moving your head and the image changing on your screen is more than about 15 milliseconds, your brain won't accept the image in front of it as "reality." Modern smartphones, though, have very powerful built-in graphics processors, allowing for the smooth creation of virtual reality content.

One thing researchers have learned is that a convincing virtual reality headset needs to provide users with a full 180-degree field of vision. If

A *gyroscope* measures your phone's orientation; the *accelerometer*, as the name suggests, measures acceleration.

you can see the edge of the headset, for example, you will never feel fully immersed. That's hard to do with a smartphone whose screen generally isn't even as wide as your head, but there are a few tricks that can widen that field of view. That's where your smartphone VR viewer's lenses come in. Indeed, when you break your viewer down to its basics, it's essentially a box purpose-built for these biconvex lenses. All of the work creating the images you see is happening on your smartphone, but without the lenses, the experience wouldn't be possible.

When you look at the images produced by Cardboard apps without the viewer, you'll notice that they are slightly distorted. That's on purpose. The images are tuned to the lenses in the headset, which create that 180-degree field of view. Every virtual reality viewer, though, has to strike a balance. You want the best possible picture, of course, but for that the VR lenses would have to be tuned to the *exact* distance between every user's eyes. That wasn't an option for the Cardboard viewer. But the headset creators believe they have found the sweet spot between ease of use, a wide field of view, and an almost undistorted image.

While the lenses are what make the VR experience possible, another ingenious trick in the original Google Cardboard device's design is the magnetic trigger button on the side. (Unfortunately, not all phones will respond to magnetic trigger pulls, and your viewer may use a different input method.) One magnet on the inside of the viewer is fixed in position with another on the outside that you can slide down. When designing the viewer, the Cardboard team experimented with a number of ways users could interact with their devices, since the touchscreen is hard to reach when the phone is in the viewer. In a funny coincidence, two team members independently came up with the same solution: a movable magnet on the side of the box. Why does that work? Because one of the many sensors in your phone is a magnetometer (which measures the magnetic field around your device). To see it at work, just open up a compass app. There are a number of other apps that use the information from this sensor, but none have used it in the way Cardboard can.

The magnets are strong, so when you pull the outer magnet down, the magnetometer notices a sudden shift in the magnetic field and passes that information on to the Cardboard app. Now the app knows that you've moved the trigger—just as your computer knows when you've clicked a mouse button or tapped a touchscreen.

You may have also noticed a small sticker on your cardboard viewer. While it might look like just an ordinary sticker, it's actually the viewer's NFC (near-field communication) tag. Google created a set of instructions for those manufacturing their own cardboard viewers (like DODOcase) so they can store various bits of information on the tag. Every cardboard viewer is a little bit different, after all, so an NFC tag could store information about the lenses, allowing the software to adjust how it displays images.

All of those parts—the smartphone sensors and screen, lenses, magnet, and NFC tag—come together to provide a compelling virtual reality experience. There are, however, some physical limitations to what's possible with this technology today.

If you use the VR viewer for too long, it can potentially make you feel slightly dizzy. To trick our brains into believing that we are in an alternate reality, the images must perfectly align with our movements. If they are even a little bit off, our brains can get confused by trying to reconcile our movements with what our eyes are seeing. Because there can be a slight lag between the moment the phone's sensors register our movement and the moment the application creates an image reacting to that movement, our brains may notice that something isn't quite right.

Google's Cardboard team recommends that if you are prone to things like motion sickness when watching 3D movies, for example, it's probably best to sit down when using your viewer. There has been some research suggesting that women are more susceptible than men to feeling dizzy in virtual reality. Why this might be is unclear, but no matter your gender, be careful and stay safe!

With the VR viewer kit and a slew of free apps from Google and other developers, you can use your smartphone to fly through Google Earth and feel like you are gliding over your favorite city. You can explore the globe, take a ride through the streets of Paris, or hop on an awesome roller coaster. Not bad for a piece of corrugated cardboard and two lenses. And it's a testament to how far technology—especially smartphone technology—has come over the past few years.

Getting Started With Your VR Viewer

Putting your cardboard VR viewer together is pretty straightforward: Just follow the instructions at **dodocase.com/vrkit1.** No special tools are necessary.

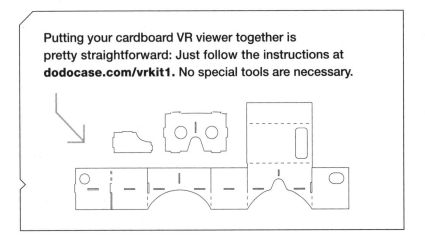

Android

To have the best initial experience with VR on an Android phone, download the DODOcase Virtual Reality app from the Google Play store. This app has the most up-to-date list of the best VR apps for Android and information on other VR-related hardware. If you are using an Apple, Windows, or other mobile device, skip forward to the iPhone section on page 17. The viewer and apps work best with Android 4.2 or iOS 7 and above.

The viewer includes a built-in NFC tag, enabling phones that have an NFC reader to automatically enter VR mode when the phone is inserted into the viewer. When your phone gets close to the NFC tag, it will launch the DODOcase Virtual Reality app and read information about your viewer's lenses and construction from the tag. This information helps virtual reality apps customize their displays for the best possible VR experience. If your phone is not responding to the NFC tag, check that you have the NFC function turned on in your phone's settings. If your phone does not have an NFC reader, you can manually launch the DODOcase Virtual Reality app from your phone's home screen before inserting it into the viewer.

The best introduction to VR for Android is the Google Cardboard app. You can find it easily through the DODOcase Virtual Reality app. Once you install and launch the Google Cardboard app, the fun begins.

Using the Google Cardboard App

When looking through the viewer, you'll see the Cardboard app's main menu, which will display all the different applications available. Move your head left or right to highlight the menu options. To launch the highlighted option, simply look at it and click the selector button on your viewer (like how you'd use a computer mouse or touchpad). Start with Cardboard's interactive "Tutorial" option, which will provide quick and easy instructions on how to navigate the app.

There are several ways to engage with the Cardboard viewer. The selector button on your VR viewer may be a ring-shaped magnet slider or some

An NFC tag is essentially a high-tech version of the anti-theft tags used in clothing stores. Instead of beeping if you leave a store with a pilfered article of clothing, the VR viewer's NFC chip stores a small amount of information that your phone can read when in close proximity to the chip. Almost all Android and Windows phones produced after 2012 have NFC readers.

other button-like mechanism. If your VR viewer has a ring slider but the app does not respond when it is pulled, your phone may not have the required magnetic sensor. Instead, you can double-tap on the phone screen through the viewer's nose opening. To get back to the main menu from elsewhere in the app, rotate the viewer clockwise 90 degrees. This is like hitting the home button on your phone.

These instructions are specific to the Google Cardboard app, and you may need to interact with other VR apps differently. Some applications use a time-delay mechanism (stare at an icon for a few seconds to open it), while others may require additional hardware, like a Bluetooth game controller.

The **CARDBOARD APP** comes with seven preloaded applications, including an interactive animated story and a flying simulator that uses Google Earth to let you fly across the world like a superhero.

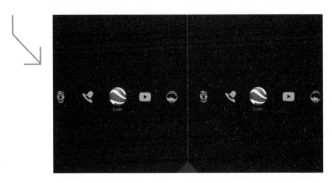

Let's take a closer look at the different apps:

GOOGLE EARTH: When you first start the Google Earth app, you'll be dropped in a random location, where you can then explore your surroundings. That by itself is pretty cool, but if you click the selector button on the cardboard viewer, you'll start moving. Look left or right, up or down, and you will begin flying in that direction. Look all the way up and the app will ask if you want to fly into space. Click the selector button again and you'll be teleported above the Earth. Look around and you'll see all the different sights Google has preselected for you. See one you like? Look at it, click the selector button again, and you'll fly there!

TOUR GUIDE: This is your chance to take a short narrated tour through the opulent Palace of Versailles—without the long journey to get there. You will experience its ornate architecture, tour its extensive art collection, and learn its fascinating history. Even if you are not a history buff, Tour Guide demonstrates the enormous experiential and educational potential of virtual reality tours.

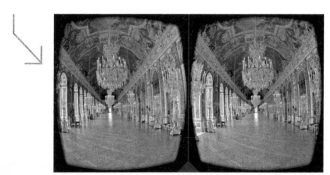

STREET VUE: The Cardboard concept was developed by a Google engineer at the company's Cultural Institute in Paris. And just like Tour Guide, Street Vue has a distinctly French flavor. Using Google Street View imagery, the app will take you on a whirlwind ride through the City of Light. The car navigates a set course, guiding you through many of Paris's major sites as if you were sitting on one of those double-decker tour buses (only this one drives quite a bit faster, is free, and isn't full of tourists).

WINDY DAY: Over the past few years, Google—specifically, its Advanced Technology and Projects (ATAP) unit, acquired from Motorola in 2011—has collaborated with animators and storytellers to determine how to best tell stories online. Windy Day was one of its projects. It was created and directed by Jan Pinkava, codirector of Pixar's hit film *Ratatouille*. We're not going to spoil the story for you, but keep an eye on the red hat.

EXHIBIT: This app breaks most of the conventional wisdom around virtual reality, providing a different experience from that found in the more traditional, immersive apps. Exhibit lets you closely examine a series of 3D renderings of historical objects, but instead of walking around them—or seeing them from one point of view, as in the Tour Guide app—you can move the object simply by moving your head. It's hard for a written description to do it justice. Give it a try and see!

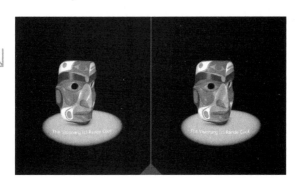

YOUTUBE: Want to watch online videos on a giant screen using a futuristic interface? Here is your opportunity! Just navigate to Cardboard's YouTube app to turn ordinary videos into an immersive viewing experience.

PHOTO SPHERE: You probably already know that you can use your Android camera app's Photo Sphere feature to take 360-degree panoramic images. Until now, the only way to really experience these photos was by using your phone's touchscreen. But with Photo Sphere for Cardboard, you can step right into them, creating your own virtual reality content by pulling images directly from your phone. So go ahead and snap a few photo spheres!

The Cardboard app will be your main gateway into virtual reality, but it's not the only way to use your new viewer. The Google Cardboard team is making it easy for Android developers to write new virtual reality applications, so over time, you will see quite a few of them appear in the DODOcase Virtual Reality app, Google's Play Store, and across the web. Indeed, a number of video game developers are hard at work creating virtual reality content and consider the technology to be the next major innovation in gaming and media.

Google itself has created a number of bonus virtual reality experiences, available through its Chrome web browser. This may seem strange, given that you probably wouldn't think of a browser as an effective way to deliver an immersive adventure in virtual reality, but over the past few years, Google and others have built advanced 3D capabilities into their browsers.

Head to **G.CO/CHROMEVR** with your mobile Chrome browser and find a number of experimental apps, including a helicopter ride over the Great

Barrier Reef; a stomach-turning trip up, down, and around a roller coaster; and a cool little coin-collecting 3D game. Those feeling nostalgic can check out the classic stereoscope toy to be immersed in historical 3D images.

Google expects developers to write even more web-based applications for Cardboard, so keep an eye out for an ever-expanding roster of third-party apps.

iPhone

At its first release, the official Google Cardboard app did not support Apple's iOS devices. But don't worry—you can still experience the magic of virtual reality on your iPhone! If you have iOS 8, your Safari browser should work with Google's Chrome VR experiments site, **G.CO/CHROMEVR**. If you are using iOS7 or older, check out these apps to get started:

THE HEIGHT: Scramble over futuristic scaffolding to collect as many items as possible. To start, look down to align the mark in the center of the screen with the icon at your feet—and off you go! Your movement tracks where you are looking, so move quickly to avoid falling off the scaffold. It's fun to play this immersive game while sitting in a swivel chair.

DIVE CITY ROLLER COASTER: Ride a roller coaster through a richly detailed virtual city. To get the full VR experience, make sure to select "3D mode" before you play.

Other iOS apps to look for include the Dive Unity Headtracker, a basic look at the fundamentals of moving around in virtual space, and Refugio3D Space Station, an exploration of a planet from outer space.

In these early days of smartphone VR, your best bet to find new apps is the Apple App Store. Note that some iPhone interactions may require tapping on the screen or using an external Bluetooth game controller or keyboard.

In time, the iPhone might offer a version of the official Google Cardboard app and support the NFC tag function of the VR viewer. Certainly, as more developers become familiar with virtual reality and 3D toolkits, you can expect to find ever more apps available for iOS.

To stay on top of VR news and the latest apps for Android and Apple smartphones, check out the "Resources" section at the back of this book or visit dodocase.com/vrkit1.

From Hype to Cardboard

So how did we get to the point where our phones can transport us into alternate worlds? Even though we have long dreamed of stepping into a computer-created "reality," consumer VR applications have long seemed tantalizingly close to the mainstream but far from usable (or affordable). So what changed?

Early attempts at virtual reality were clumsy because computers were still slow and expensive—limiting the pool of VR tinkerers—and computer-graphics technology was rudimentary. But that didn't stop researchers in the 1960s from giving it a try. The most famous early attempt at a virtual reality viewer was Ivan Sutherland's 1965 "Ultimate Display." There were no high-resolution LED displays at the time, and computer graphics were still in their infancy, but Sutherland and his team were able to create basic wireframes of the technology. It was a scary-looking contraption, with a headset suspended from a frame that could register movement.

"The Ultimate Display would, of course, be a room within which the computer can control the existence of matter," Sutherland wrote. "A chair displayed in such a room would be good enough to sit in." Even today, this remains the holy grail of virtual reality. (After all, what he describes is basically the *Star Trek* holodeck.) Despite all the massive leaps in technological advances since the 1960s, Google Cardboard—and any other virtual reality viewer or helmet—can show what that room looks like, but the user can't manipulate objects within that room.

Sutherland would go on to revolutionize many aspects of computer graphics, but it wouldn't be until the 1980s that computers were powerful enough to make the dream of virtual reality seem achievable. (NASA started taking it seriously, as did the U.S. military.) But even then, the hardware available to researchers made the graphics look basic by today's hyper-realistic standards.

By the late 1980s, as personal computers became more affordable and mainstream, "virtual reality" became one of the most overused buzzwords in the tech industry. It was already heralded as revolutionary, and plenty of ink was spilled on topics like the "metaphysics of virtual reality" and what communication would look like in this soon-to-be age of virtual reality.

William Gibson's popular science-fiction novel *Neuromancer* did its part to popularize the concept in the 1980s, as did Neal Stephenson's 1992 book *Snow Crash*. But science-fiction writers had long thought about realities that only existed inside a computer.

By the mid-1990s—just as the Internet was becoming mainstream and, with it, the idea of a "cyberspace"—virtual reality again became a hot topic. Both Nintendo and Sega tried to release virtual reality headsets with built-in consoles. Sega's system never went to market, but Nintendo pressed forward. The company's Virtual Boy had an odd red LED screen but didn't really qualify as a headset. Instead, it sat on a tripod. The early reviews were relentlessly negative, and the device's few users complained of headaches and dizziness. Nintendo had so hyped the Virtual Boy that its failure didn't just spell doom for the project, it also cast a pall over the idea of virtual reality as an accessible consumer technology.

Some arcade games at the time—which often included custom-built hardware with significantly more power than the average consumer device— also experimented with virtual reality, but building them was prohibitively expensive, and the decline of the arcade industry quickly put a halt to the VR experiments.

With the failure of the Virtual Boy and excessive media hype—which in the technology industry is inevitably followed by a backlash—you can see why "virtual reality" became something of a dirty word in the tech world. And from the mid-1990s to just recently, virtual reality remained relegated to niche uses in the medical field and among industrial designers and architects. Various branches of the U.S. military have used virtual reality to prepare soldiers for the battlefield, while other government organizations have experimented with it in the creation of disaster-preparedness programs.

These projects sustained a low level of interest in virtual reality, but after the early failures, few large consumer-technology companies wanted to be associated with it. At the same time, most of the hype—and venture capital—in the technology industry was flowing to software and Internet projects. So even if a startup *wanted* to attempt to reboot consumer virtual reality, it would likely have had a difficult time securing the necessary funds to do so. While there were VR headsets available during this time, they were expensive and of variable quality.

It really wasn't until inventor Palmer Luckey started Oculus VR and developed a headset called the Oculus Rift that people regained interest in the concept of humans inhabiting computer-generated realities. Luckey always had a deep interest in all things VR, and over the years he amassed one of the largest private collections of virtual reality headsets in the world. But none of the existing technologies provided him with the feeling of immersion he was looking for. So he developed his own. In many ways, Luckey's is the story of an industry outsider who didn't know that something couldn't be done. But he arrived on the scene just as hardware startups were getting hot again. Within a few days of the announcement of the Oculus Rift, Luckey's Kickstarter campaign saw a staggering $1 million in preorders and reached $2.4 million in preorders in just one month. The device was a such a hit at the annual E3 games convention in 2013 that John Carmack, the inventor of classic video games like *Doom* and *Quake*, signed on to become the CTO of the company.

In early 2014, Facebook acquired Oculus VR for $2 billion. With the imprimatur of Mark Zuckerberg, virtual reality was suddenly hot again. And now Sony is working on a VR headset for its PlayStation console, Microsoft is rumored to be working on a similar project for its Xbox, and Oculus is still going strong. (A *Wired* magazine writer recently demoed an Oculus Rift game that was "so real it nearly destroyed me.")

Projects like the Virtual Boy had obviously arrived too early. The available technology was no match for Nintendo's ambition. But the smartphone you put into the cardboard viewer is infinitely more powerful than any desktop computer of the 1990s. Indeed, it has more powerful graphics chips than many computers had just a few years ago, and its screen likely has a higher resolution than your current desktop computer or the HDTV hanging on the wall of your living room. It's these dizzying advances in technology—which have allowed for faster and more complex computing devices at a fraction of the cost—that make a project like Google Cardboard possible.

So where does Cardboard fit into the story of VR? The project is the brainchild of David Coz, an engineer at the Google Cultural Institute in Paris. Google famously gives most of its engineers what it calls "20 percent time," during which they are allowed to expend one-fifth of their working week on a passion project outside of their day-to-day responsibilities. Coz's extracurricular interest was virtual reality, with a particular focus on using smartphones to introduce VR to a wider audience. He began building prototype viewers out of cardboard because it was an easy—and cheap—material to work with.

During a trip to Google's headquarters in Mountain View, California, he showed his prototype to Christian Plagemann, a senior researcher with Google Research. Plagemann loved the idea and passed it around to other engineers in the company, as well as Google CEO Larry Page.

Coz's project arrived on the Google campus at just the right time. Every year, Google holds a large developer conference in San Francisco, and the company typically gives away a couple of cool gadgets to every audience member. Page was so enamored with the idea of Cardboard that he gave the go-ahead to develop the project—and make it the gift given to every attendee of that year's conference.

Within a few weeks, Plagemann and Coz had assembled a team of engineers and "20 percenters" from around the company to turn his prototype into an actual product—and to build enough units to be handed out at the event. Plagemann's team worked with other groups at Google, too, to create the software platform and VR experiences that are now part of the Cardboard app. The Google Maps team, for example, built the Google Earth VR experience, while a few engineers from the YouTube team built the YouTube VR app. With all these resources being harnessed, the development process only took about eight weeks and was completed in time for the company's July 2014 developer conference. Cardboard was one of the biggest surprises of the show.

Charting VR's Future

Think of VR today as radio in 1920, television in 1939, or the Internet in 1991, just when these emerging technologies were reaching a commercial tipping point, on the verge of disrupting and remaking the media landscape. Just as television added a visual dimension to the sound of radio, virtual reality adds a third dimension to the flat, two-dimensional screens of computers and televisions. And with VR, we are on the cusp of the next major media and technology transformation.

If history is any guide, mainstream adoption of VR will happen quickly. One need only look at major shifts of the past century (radio, TV, Internet) and measure the time from a technology's first consumer availability to its widespread adoption. In fact, we can spot a consistent historical pattern: Every new leap in media technology reaches 50 million people roughly *three times* faster than the technology that preceded it.

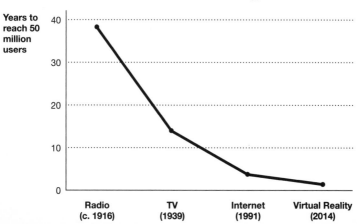

20th Century Media and Technology Transitions

Let's take a closer look at each of these major media shifts, paying particular attention to how quickly they became mainstream and what the technology cost when first introduced to consumers.

Radio: Thirty-eight years to reach 50 million users. Radio added speed to communication and sound to the written word. The first consumer radios hit the market in 1920, costing anywhere from $25 to $325 ($300 to $4,000 in 2014 dollars).

Television: Fourteen years to reach 50 million users. TV added a visual dimension to the sound of radio. The first consumer TV was sold in 1939 for $600 ($10,000 in 2014 dollars).

Internet: Four years to reach 50 million users. The Internet added a dimension of speed and interactivity to communication. On August 6, 1991, the World Wide Web was made available to the public for the first time. At the time, Apple's Macintosh Classic was one of the world's most popular PCs, costing $1,000 to $1,500 ($1,700 to $2,600 in 2014 dollars).

Virtual Reality: DODOcase predicts that it will take a year and a half from the fall of 2014 to reach 50 million virtual reality users. VR adds a dimension of immersion to the interactivity of the Internet and the flat 2D screen experience. What does it cost? Around $25 and a smartphone you very likely already own.

You might be saying to yourself, "That's crazy! How could VR spread that fast?" Well, imagine it is 1939 and instead of spending $600 on a television, you could drop your radio into a $1.38 magic box that turned it *into* a TV? Your smartphone VR viewer is that magic box.

Radio, television, and the Internet all suffered from a lack of content when they first became available to consumers. Naturally, this slowed their

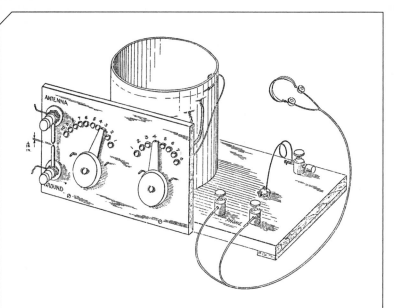

The DIY spirit of Google Cardboard's virtual reality viewer can be found in the early days of radio. In the 1920s, many radio listeners built their own receivers from plans printed in *Circular No. 120—Construction and Operation of a Very Simple Radio Receiving Equipment,* published by the U.S. Department of Commerce's Bureau of Standards. Interestingly, one of the main components of the DIY radio, the "Tuning Coil," was a cylindrical cardboard oatmeal box!

adoption. If you wanted to make content for radio or television, you needed government permission to lay wires or broadcast radio frequencies—huge investments requiring huge risks. Today, there are hundreds of thousands of mobile-app and web developers making great content from their living rooms, distributing it on the Internet without regulation or massive expense. Think of all the 3D animated movies and games that already exist. These can be ported to virtual reality with relative ease.

With a low barrier to entry for consumers (your cardboard viewer), ease of content creation, and a solid foundation of previously built technology, fast adoption of virtual reality seems not only possible but likely.

There can be little doubt that virtual reality is here to stay. And while few people have seen VR in action, projects like the Cardboard viewer provide easy, affordable, and hands-on experience with the technology—spurring more companies into creating more powerful hardware devices and more complex software experiences.

But for now, put your phone into your viewer and lose yourself in a virtual world. You just might be peering into the future.

Q&A with the Google Cardboard Team

*Christian Plagemann is a senior research scientist at Google. He focuses on interaction research and has a PhD in robotics. He has previously worked on autonomous cars and currently studies how humans interact with computers without using a keyboard and mouse. **Andrew Nartker** is a product manager with Google Docs and Drive and is also the product manager for the Cardboard project.*

How did this project get started?

CHRISTIAN: The idea originally came from David Coz, who is a software engineer in France at the Google Cultural Institute. He developed this in his free time, parallel to his job. He just had the idea of bringing virtual reality to everyone and worked on Cardboard with his friend Damien Henry. He was on a business trip to Google headquarters in Mountain View and started showing this around. I thought this was absolutely amazing.

We discussed it in a larger group and came up with the idea to scale it up a notch and give it to developers at Google I/O. Many "20 percenters" across the company joined the project on short notice. We quickly got interest from higher-ups, and they said, "Let's do this."

I/O is Google's annual conference for developers in San Francisco.

How do you reach the people "high up" at Google?

CHRISTIAN: Oh, it was easy. The thing is, Google is not very hierarchical. Projects don't go from manager to manager to manager for approval, especially at Google Research. We showed the prototype to Alan Eustace and Sundar Pichai, and then we got to Larry Page really quickly. They are always very interested in new stuff. We showed it to Larry and said, "Hey, you have to see this." It was very casual. The response was, "This is amazing, you should do it."

Sundar Pichai is Google's SVP of Android, Chrome & Apps. Larry Page is one of Google's founders and its CEO.

ANDREW: Because Google has so many bottom-up ideas from experts in their fields, often product management comes in and helps us figure out what to prioritize. With Cardboard, we could've done so many different things, so we worked out a nice, simple product that we could deliver in a compressed time frame. The process was very informal. People joined in and dropped out as they had time. The whole project took six to eight weeks.

CHRISTIAN: During that time, obviously, it was very intense work. But on the other hand, it was easy to get people to donate their time and sweat. We expected we would finish two or three demos, but in the end, there were seven super-nice demos.

The main reason was that the team, led by Leandro Gracia, developed a really solid library foundation and a very simple demo app. It was actually the Cultural Institute, YouTube, Google Earth, Maps, and Windy Day teams who said, "Hey, our content would fit really well." With that, we had a bit of internal competition, and everybody gave their best.

Did you reject any ideas?

CHRISTIAN: The expectation definitely was that we would try all these different things, and in the end we'd throw out the ones that weren't good. We had two or three ideas we didn't pursue, but in the end, most projects that got built ended up in the app.

ANDREW: We set a very high bar for quality. Even though we wanted this to be a playful thing, we knew that we were entering a very new space with VR, and we wanted to put our best foot forward as Google. We wanted to make sure that people understand that virtual reality can be really good. We wanted to make great experiences without gimmicky components. So we challenged all the teams to actually make the best experience possible, and everybody stepped up. We set a couple of guidelines and standards and did some coaching with our industry experts, and everybody just took to it.

CHRISTIAN: That was actually very important for us. The entire approach was scrappy, but it was important that the experience would be really good. At the same time, we didn't want this to appear like a final, polished product.

Why didn't you want it to look like a polished product?

CHRISTIAN: We wanted it to be very honest and open, and that's why we kept the cardboard feel to it. It was a really fun "20 percent" project, not a product.

ANDREW: We wanted this to appeal to the makers, developers, and hackers. We built it for ourselves, really. Cardboard just stuck as a very solid basis to design from.

CHRISTIAN: There was discussion internally whether we should make this from plastic or use other materials, or maybe coat it. But we agreed that we wanted it to be simple, and we wanted people to be able to build their own.

We wanted this to be a blueprint that Google would put out into the world and that we would stand behind, but that everybody could take and then make other experiences based on it. We want others to innovate on top of what we built.

How did we get to this point where we can build something like Cardboard?

ANDREW: Smartphones are pushing the miniaturization of performance of computing, opening up all these new capabilities. This is a clear example. We took what's good about smartphones to create an immersive experience, with a great screen and sensors to teleport you into a different world.

CHRISTIAN: If you look at the cost of smartphones—the majority is I/O. It used to be that the major cost of your computer was the actual core—the processor, the memory—but the major costs for phones today are the touchscreen, the WiFi, the sensors. The user experience has become the major defining factor of our devices. I think the VR experience is an example of this.

Does using the smartphone limit what you can do?

CHRISTIAN: There is a large variety of phones of different qualities. Obviously, there are devices where the tracking isn't that precise and where there is substantial latency between orientation tracking and the rendering pipeline. If you compare this to the super-optimized, high-end VR solutions, latency is naturally higher. That's one of the limitations, but not a principal limitation. It's just a consequence of the fact that device manufacturers haven't been tracking these kinds of things. These devices could have perfect orientation tracking, but device manufacturers never had to solve this before.

> I/O stands for input/output, or the different ways to get information in and out of a computer or smartphone.

ANDREW: A lot of people are circling around these hardware limitations and quickly solving them at different price points. It's flipping to these new challenges. You can imagine, once you have this thing on your face, how do you start to interact with it? How do you as a developer make experiences and stories for it? That's kind of like what we are doing. The pieces are in place, and people are now thinking about how to make stories.

A lot of the experiences you see today were taken off the shelf and are coming from a different world. They weren't built for VR, for 3D stereoscopic rendering right next to your face. And so now we are trying to figure out how you design uniquely for this; developers and storytellers are learning.

CHRISTIAN: One thing we learned is that you don't have to have perfectly low latency. You can still create interesting apps, for example, by avoiding rapid camera accelerations. In Windy Day, there is no translational motion, and you can just look around. In that setting, there is no walking, but the user experience is nevertheless great. For a video experience, if you don't glue the video to your face, when you let the screen stay in absolute space and you move your head around, it's a much, much better experience than when the screen is glued to your face.

ANDREW: A lot of people are still learning how to design these immersive experiences.

CHRISTIAN: Another thing we learned was that virtual reality doesn't need to be realistic. State-of-the-art knowledge in the space has been that there has to be a physically realistic virtual environment around you. One thing we discovered was that this doesn't have to be the case at all. The Exhibit demo, for example, moves in an unrealistic way—it hovers in front of you and rotates with your head orientation—but it works extremely well. The launcher is a similar thing. The elements move at a faster pace than you are moving your head.

There is this uncanny valley between the rather abstract experiences and reality. When you get closer to reality—but not quite—that's where you get some problems and people can get sick. If you stay further away, in an abstract space, or you get *really, really* close to reality, you're fine. If you design applications with the state of the tech in mind, you can stay out of this valley in either direction. But there are some applications, no matter what platform, that don't work.

If I "accelerate" the user really fast, for example by throwing him down a roller coaster, the result won't be great. There are just physical effects to this. If you see acceleration that your body isn't experiencing, you will feel this mismatch. In Google Earth, obviously we want people to get around, and the way we implemented this was that we only translate in viewing direction, and relatively slowly. You can fly—but only forward. When you move your head, you can fly sideways, but we never accelerate you sideways. When you want to transition to farther-away places, we let you look to these hot spots and then beam you to them.

We are still in the very early days of VR. There is so much stuff still to happen and to figure out around interactions and experiences to see what works and what doesn't. Like external tracking, where you can have full 360-degree tracking, or see-through augmented reality experiences. The platforms will become better and better.

That's exactly why we chose the open approach. We want to enable as many people as possible to start working on this. We want to have a platform that people can use as a benchmark. You can put the same app on different phones and you can directly compare.

What about the different parts of Cardboard besides the smartphone? The NFC tag, the lenses, and the magnet? What's the story behind those?

CHRISTIAN: We can use the NFC chip to store the exact optics and capabilities of the device, and we can preconfigure the software. The moment you touch the NFC chip, the phone knows about the optical setup and the calibration and what the device can do. Then it can automatically configure the experience. That way you could use a different viewer and the phone can read the information about it. We are in the process of open-sourcing the code.

So you could optimize for a specific screen. The phone knows everything about its own screen, but it doesn't know about the viewer and the lenses, etc. If you know that as well, you can optimize the entire rendering pipeline for that viewer. That enables people to come up with their own viewers, sparing the user from having to select which viewer they are using right now, for example, or go through a specific calibration step.

What about the magnet?

CHRISTIAN: Two people in the group—Boris Smus and Hendrik Dahlkamp— invented this overnight. At the same time. We sat around brainstorming ideas on interaction. Everybody was thinking, and we were trying different things. And then two of our people came up with the same idea. And so we thought, okay, that's a good indication. So we tried it out, and within a few days, we had it working.

We use the magnetometer in the phone to detect whether the magnet is moving or not. It's a bit tricky. All the different phones have slightly different sensors and slightly different calibration mechanisms. One of the things that all phones have is a compass self-calibration. Depending on which environment you are in and how close you are to metal, the compass can be off. So they try to calibrate the sensor over time. The hard part was to deal with all of these different calibration behaviors across phones. Some do it gradually over a longer period of time time, some wait for a while and then have a big calibration event.

Your team also spent a lot of time on deciding which lenses to use, right?

CHRISTIAN: The lens was a difficult question. We tried to find the sweet spot between having very high accuracy—where you have a very wide field of view and a very clear picture—and on the other extreme wanting this to be extremely easy to use use, where you hold it up to your face and it just works. The lens and setup we chose is kind of the sweet spot between the two. If you go with a really high field of view, you end up with a lot of distortion, and you have to adapt the lenses to your eyes. We didn't want that. We wanted it to be very simple, where this worked for everyone, so we went with lenses that don't distort too much but still have as wide a field of view as possible.

In principle, these are really cheap lenses. They are made of plastic.

How can developers write new applications for Cardboard?

CHRISTIAN: They can write Android apps. If you can write an OpenGL app, you can as easily write a virtual reality–enabled app. Our framework creates two cameras and places them at the right interocular distance in space. We do the head tracking and the placement of the camera, and then we just run your rendering routine twice, once for each eye.

What about porting existing applications?
Are there apps out there that have done this?

CHRISTIAN: It's not hard. We tried to give developers different levels of granularity. We can just render it for you, or you can have more powerful access where you are in charge of rendering the entire screen. Or if you want to do orientation tracking yourself, you can do that. Or do the rendering yourself, we allow you to do that, too.

Alternatively, you can build pretty compelling VR experiences in any WebGL-enabled mobile browser.

Still, it's pretty hard for mainstream users to
go in and create their own virtual reality experiences.

CHRISTIAN: It's always been a chicken and egg problem. Very few devices, very few developers, very few use cases. It's kind of this vicious circle. That's why we chose this open and broad approach to bootstrap the process, so more people can get this viewing experience in an inexpensive way. So we actually hope that many more authoring tools will get built for this kind of experience. We should make it easier for people to build this stuff.

What's the future of the project at Google?
Are people still working on it?

CHRISTIAN: There are people contributing to it and lots of people thinking about driving it forward. We're working on supporting developers, but this is very early in this entire topic. We are definitely taking feedback on how it works on different devices and what people want to do with it, and we're improving the library.

Resources

We are at the beginning of a virtual reality revolution. The devices, apps, and websites that you can use to experiment with VR are under continual development, so keep checking in.

dodocase.com/vrkit1
Your portal to the world of VR through your smartphone

cardboardapps.com
An unofficial repository of information and demo apps for Google Cardboard

g.co/cardboard
The official Google Cardboard site

g.co/chromevr
The official Google Cardboard Chrome VR experiments site

bit.ly/WRCcRU
The Cardboard Google+ community site

reddit.com/r/GoogleCardboard
Reddit's Cardboard community

divegames.com
A source for 3D VR games